BLOWING OUT THE CANDLES

A POETRY TRILOGY

BY

JAMES PAUL GEE

BLOWING OUT THE CANDLES

A POETRY TRILOGY

BY

JAMES PAUL GEE

GARN PRESS

NEW YORK, NY

GARN PRESS

NEW YORK, NY

Published by Garn Press, LLC
New York, NY
www.garnpress.com

Book cover photo by Ben James Taylor/Garn Press
Book and cover design by Ben James Taylor/Garn Press
Book illustrations by Malia Hughes

Library of Congress Control Number: 2013949938

Publisher's Cataloging-in-Publication Data
Gee, James Paul.
Blowing out the candles trilogy / James Paul Gee.
    p. cm.
  ISBN: 978-0-9899106-3-7 (pbk.)
  ISBN: 978-0-9899106-0-6 (e-book one)
  ISBN: 978-0-9899106-1-3 (e-book two)
  ISBN: 978-0-9899106-2-0 (e-book three)
1. Philosophy—Poetry. 2. World politics—Poetry. 3.
American poetry—21st century.   I. Title. II. Series: Blowing out the candles.
  PS3607.E3613 B55 2013
    811—dc23
                  2013949938

For Bead

Table of Contents

Introduction

When Stravinsky's Rite of Spring was first performed at the Théâtre des Champs Elysées in Paris, people in the audience started shouting and fighting. In an audio recording one woman who was in the theatre at the time says she saw a lady lean over the side of her box and hit the man in the next box with her umbrella. Stravinsky was in the audience that night, and so were Gertrude Stein and Pablo Picasso. Stravinsky is reported to have left the theatre in dismay before the end of the performance. Later, when asked about the Rite of Spring, Stravinsky said he did not sit and compose the music in the usual way, but that it came to him, as if it was written. If that is what happened, he did not make up the tonality, the meter, the stress, or the dissonance, it was already there, and Stravinsky must have experienced one of those rare lucid moments when the unconscious and conscious unite.

In Healing the Soul in the Age of the Brain, Elio Frattaroli explores such moments, and he writes about what happens when our inner selves become entwined with our public persona of self. Emphasizing with italics, he states, "the fear of consciousness is ultimately a fear of moral responsibility". For most of us those lucid moments, often between dreaming and waking, that Stravinsky experienced and of which Frattaroli writes, don't amount to much. Our inclination is to turn over and go back to sleep. But sometimes, when a person has spent his life pursuing a life of scholarly work and deep contemplation, if such a lucid moment comes when he hears music or poetry, however strident or dissonant or melodic, whatever the text, and however raw and revealing it may be, he writes it down and does not fear it. This is my understanding of how

Jim Gee wrote his poems.

"These poems came to me when they—yes, the poems themselves—told me to invite them in," Gee explains. "I don't know why."

He says he doesn't know where the poems came from. They arrived it would seem, like Stravinsky's Rite of Spring, only for Gee the "rite" comes in the winter, in the midst of his aging discontent.

"People get old at different ages, some quite young," Gee says. "This stage-to-nowhere phase of life we call old age makes you think."

Sometimes cynical, sometimes searing, at times gut wrenching, the poems are of heart and mind, filled with pathos and humor. They have the power to turn us inside out, and make us think about our own lives, about our relationships with each other, about our covenants with religion, and about our passivity in dealing with governments and bureaucracies. Sometimes he is strident and in our face, but Gee cares for us enough to take us into his life space. In an act of courage, he takes off his armor, and brutally honest, he peels back the layers, until all contrivance has left him and he appears before us vulnerable on the page. These are poems not only for quiet contemplation, but also poems to be shared.

"I have spent my career as an academic," Gee tells us. "When I was young, to me being an academic meant being a secular priest. But my church is a fallen church. We no longer honor little things like truth, but only big things like money."

There is enough about the poems to keep a conversation going in a class in the Humanities or Sciences for an entire semester, and the issues raised about the politics and ethics of representation, the demands of official ideology, and the inexplicable human capacity for good and evil, are more than enough to keep us all conscious of the increasing dehumanization of the age we live in.

"All of us humans think, feel, and speak in poetry when we hurt," Gee continues. "Prick us, do we not all bleed in pulses and rhythms, in metaphors and pleas? When we drop pretense, we are incensed as humans at unfairness. We are incensed at anyone being left out, put down, or left to drown in sorrow."

If all this sounds too heavy, it is important to add – at the risk of Gee's wrath – that his poems will also make you laugh. They are paradoxical as well as quixotic, filled with the absurdities of life that make good stories to share with friends over coffee or dinner. I have done just that, for sometimes in our lives when our unconscious and conscious meet, the cry out loud comes in the form of a laugh.

It is with great pleasure that Garn Press has now published a paperback version of Jim's poems to delight readers as well as unsettle them. This is a book that you can put in your bag and take on the bus or subway, read in a coffee shop, pull out when events happen, and read the poems again as if they are new - which they always will be, because they shine a light on our humanity.

Denny Taylor
New York, NY
January 2015

Book One

Souls

Vampires

Once, long ago, I wrote about a vampire.
Now I am a vampire.

Vampires can live forever.
Eventually they live so long they have no home.
Everything familiar has long disappeared.
They can barely recall the world in which they were born.
Some of them long for death.

All of us can be vampires now.
It used to take hundreds of years for a vampire to grow weary.
Now it takes less than a mortal's life.
One lifetime is now a thousand years of change.

Not all vampires grow weary, I suppose.
Some of us old people want to live forever.
Some of us are asking biology for eternal life.
Some of us want science to heal frayed telomeres and cure old genes.

When I was quite young, I warped in time.
I went back hundreds of years.
You could do that then.
It took guts or fear or wanting to leave home.

Ironic now, isn't it? This wanting to leave home.

In the warp, there was no radio.
No TV.
No newspapers.
No magazines.
No phones.
No family.

No girls or women either.
In fact, they gave me a little black book that said:
"All girls and women have lust in their hearts"
(This I found out much later was sadly not true).

We rose at 6:05 and went to bed at 9:05.
We slept on straw.
We ate bad food.
We ate in silence listening to one of our kind read bloody stories about
    torture.
I took my turn to read.
Sometimes we secretly waited for the delivery man and begged for bread.

The library stopped in the 18th century.
Descartes, Leibniz, and Spinoza were banned.
So they weren't there.
I found them, secretly, hidden, not in their own books.
St. Anselm had turned me on to them.
Though he didn't know it.

I did once escape the warp world.
I hid under a blanket guiltily reading Kant in a very strange place.
San Francisco.
Forbidden fruit.
Kant, too, was banned.

It was slow going, reading Kant.
Many years later I read Kant again in a philosophy course in college.
I went to my professor and said I could not be a philosopher.
I just read too slowly.
He asked me how many pages of Kant or Hegel I could read an hour.
I said two or three max.
He said "You are reading too fast".

I saw both God and the Devil in the time warp world.
God, two or three times.
The Devil, only once.
Actually I did not really see the Devil.
Someone else did and told me.
To be accurate, he was more heard than seen scratching at a window.

I discovered the Cuban Missile Crisis when I found an old
     wind-blown page of a newspaper in our forest.
It said there was a crisis.
There might be Nuclear War, it said.
I had no idea how it had all turned out.
Perhaps the world had been destroyed, save for our forest.
I looked for a later page.

I couldn't find one.

When I was very young I had a textbook called "The Evil Tree".
It was a Catholic book.
It said Communism was the Work of the Devil.
Communism would Never Die.
Russia was the Eternal Evil Empire.
We needed Eternal Vigilance.
Now Communism is gone.
The Evil Empire is Dust.
So is the Catholic Church, trapped in a tar pit of its own making.

In one fell swoop I went from the time warp world into the 60's.
It was a bigger warp to the 60's than it had been from my home to
    the warp world.
I walked right onto a Sunny beach in a Sunny college town.
There were long-haired hippies, surfers, and beautiful girls in bikinis
    the size of napkins.
When they weren't wearing nothing at all at Nude-Ins Against the War.

I came on the scene wearing a black suit, a stiff white shirt, a thin
    tie, and a crew cut.
My small British mother was with me.
The hippies, the surfers, the girls stared.
Not hostilely.
It was, after all, the 60's.
They were very nice to me.

The surfers came to trust me with their girlfriends when they were
    out cheating on them.
They knew I didn't know what to do.
I bought a book about women's bodies.
It was all line drawings.
I could make no sense of it at all.
I have always been bad with maps.

That's why today I believe in Doing before Reading.
That's why I believe in gaining images and actions before words.
Reading bodies before reading about bodies.

The Philosophy Department Head asked what I had come to study.
I said Metaphysics: Descartes, Leibniz, and Spinoza.
That's what you get when you ban things.
He said no one did Metaphysics any more.
That was all just History now.
I had arrived too late.
I had really wanted to make a contribution to Metaphysics.

I asked what THEY did now.
He said:
Analytic philosophy.
Linguistic philosophy.
Wittgenstein. Austin. Ryle.

I admitted then I had not been able to get into any classes anyway.
They were all full.
I had failed to mail back some little cards.
I hadn't known what the cards were for.
So I had stood in long lines to get courses.
But the courses were all filled by the time I got to the front.
And I had no priority.
I had been in the warp world too long.

The Department Head said all that was left was his Plato class.
But it was a graduate class.
Not for undergraduates, especially not new ones.
I was desperate.
"Could he help me?"
I begged.
"Well, have you ever read Plato?"
Sheepishly, I said: "I have only read him in Greek".

I thought you were supposed to have read him in English.
It somehow seemed more modern. Not time warped.
In the time warp world we read Greek and Latin.
We also ate meals silently, listening to stories about torture, as I said.

He said, "You're in".
And we read Plato in English.

That ocean place and time is now long gone.
A bank got burned.
And in America you don't burn banks.
Not even way back then.

Soldiers filled the town with guns, gas canisters, and dump trucks.
A helicopter and a dump truck once made me hop on one leg back
    to my room.
I was caught in the dark after curfew.
A light shone down on me from the sky.
A voice spoke out of the light.
It told me to STOP.
I thought it was God, for the third or fourth time.
But it was the helicopter.
It told me to wait.
A dump truck full of policemen with masks and shields and guns came
    up behind me.
The helicopter told me to start hopping.
I did.

The town in which I was born is long gone now too.
Once despised, it found love when it discovered Silicon.
Those of us born there could no longer afford to live there.
It had become fancy and we had not.

I became a university professor because the time warp world had

disappeared.
The old stone buildings were torn down.
The forest was leveled.
Concrete was poured
A suburb was born.
The time warp world was buried underneath it.
There was a sign that said it had been there.
The sign may be gone now too.
Once it took hundreds or thousands of years to bury worlds.
Now one lifetime is more than enough.

The university was the closest thing I could find to the time warp world.
In the time warp world they told me that if anyone earned a PhD, he
    would lose his FAITH
(Remember, no women, so no pronoun problem).
I earned my PhD in another Sunny place.
Once, in graduate school, my main professor left to take another job.
Her name was Joan.
I felt bereft.
The new one was not coming for a semester.
His name was Tom.
I needed someone to study with.
Someone as good and special as Joan.
Not just anyone.

I shared my concern with the Department Head.
Her name was Clara.
She told me to pick anyone in the world.
Anyone.
She told me to consult with Joan.
Clara would bring whomever I chose to me.
So I could work with them while I waited for Tom.

I picked a famous professor from Paris.
His name was Richie.
Clara called him in Paris right in front of me.

When Richie came, I was the only student in both his classes.
One was a small seminar.
I had to give the first student presentation.
There were no other student presentations after that.
The other class was in an old large lecture hall.
Richie lectured from a lectern on a high wooden stage.
I sat alone in the hall, near the front, way down below.
Richie stopped every once in a while, looked down, and asked whether
    there were any questions.
Often there were.

The University is gone now too.
It is just another bank.
The ratio is not one to one.
The professors are Automatic Teller Machines, with fees.

And America is gone too.
Oh, I know I am not supposed to call it that.
I know there is a South America.
And a Central America.
Even a Canada.
But America is what we called it back then.
When it was still there.

Souls

I once wrote about the soul in an academic book.
The book is old now and out of print.
A Cambridge Puritan told me the soul was not a fit academic topic.
In any case, the soul itself is old now and out of print.

When I was young, the soul was pictured as a milk bottle.
The bottle was partly white with grace (milk) and partly black with sin.
If the milk ran out, you were filled with sin.
Mortal Sin: Big sins which can send your soul to hell.
Now I know you're just empty.

Dualism died sometime in the 20th century.
Descartes said Mind and Body were radically different.
But they are the same.
The mind is a flow of chemicals and electricity across networked neurons.

Alas, the system of networked neurons and its connections and settings
    is complex.
It is more complex than the universe.
There are more connections and settings in the brain than there are stars
    in the universe.
When Dualism collapsed, the Mind did not get any less mysterious.
It got more mysterious.

But it became the mind, not Mind anymore.

When I was a young teen, I read Descartes out loud pacing in my small
    back yard.
In those days, I pronounced his name Des-CAR-tes, not DE-cart.
I had never heard it said.
My family was not (capital "E") Educated.

Des-CAR-tes thrilled me.
Such BOLD thoughts.
To figure out the whole world in PURE THOUGHT!
Cogito Ergo Sum; "I think, therefore I am".

Later, a professor told me a better translation, philosophically, was:
"I doubt, therefore I am"; Dubito, Ergo Sum.
Now I know a better translation, philosophically, is:
"I am because I say so".
It is one of the few things that are true just because you say it.

Some people used to think Mind and Soul were the same thing.
When it was Mind and not mind.
Others didn't.
But now that the mind is chemicals, it is no longer Mind.
And the (little "m") mind can't be the Soul.
Because the Soul isn't chemicals.
Though I think it is the (little "s") soul, really, and not the Soul.
After all, even God has become god.

One of my favorite poems is "Parting".
It is a poem by Emily Dickinson.
I once taught poetry, even though I had never read any.
Except for T.S. Eliot late at night on a cold stairwell in a time warp world:

My life closed twice before its close;
It yet remains to see
If Immortality unveil
A third event to me,
So huge, so hopeless to conceive,
As these that twice befell.
Parting is all we know of heaven,
And all we need of hell.

I once lived in Emily's town.
I have been in her house.
Emily had an interesting take on religion.
She wrote her poems in the rhythm of the Protestant Hymnal.
But they are heresy through and through.

Emily's poem—I like to call her Emily, since I once wanted to date her—
    is about the soul
(Yes, I know Emily was a lesbian. I expected as much back then.
Had I had the choice of what to be, my first choice would have been to
    be a hippo.
Human is way down on my list.
But if I had to be human, I would have wanted to be a lesbian).

Emily's poem is about the soul, not the Soul.
That is one reason it's heresy.
That is one reason it's modern.
Or, maybe it is just about parting being such sweet sorrow, as Juliet said
    to Romeo.
Perhaps, though, Emily's point is that "parting is such sweet sorrow"
    is about the soul.
Life closing has always intrigued me.
It intrigues me ever more now that I am old.
Any human knows, as Emily says, that we humans can die more than once.
When I was a teenager, I knew Emily's lesson down deep in my soul.
Then I had strong feelings.
Things really truly passionately actually mattered.

Life was tasty and full of salt.
Today I am on a low salt diet.
Nonetheless, I can still die.

Emily is offering a proof of the soul.
So, her poem is, in a sense, an academic text.
A treatise on the soul.
There are two ways to die.
One can happen only once:
When the body dies.
One can happen many times:
When the soul dies.

The soul, unlike the body, can suffer mortal damage and live to die again.
The soul dies when the milk bottle is empty.
It can fill and empty again.
Emptiness isn't sin.
It's the death of the soul, the emptying of the bottle.
It is what the mystic St. John of the Cross called "The Dark Night of
　　the Soul".

I write this in my home town, Sedona, Arizona.
Red rocked Sedona is the New Age Capital of America.
I write in a coffee shop where New Age is the standard language.
Here is some New Age language I found on something called
　　"The Mystic.org":

　　"Dark night of the soul" sounds like a … much to be avoided
　　　　experience.
　　Yet … seekers on the road to higher consciousness will pass
　　　　through the dark night.
　　In fact, they may pass through several until they experience the
　　　　… joy of their true nature.
　　Many seekers would encourage the dark night experience if they
　　　　knew what it was.

However, to one engaged in the dark night, suffering
seems unending.

We humans do have a nature ("... joy of their true nature").
Human nature.
Though liberal academics don't like it.
But we do not have individual natures, like "Jim's nature".
There isn't a "true Jim" to be discovered or even made.
What you discover in the Dark Night of the Soul is not your true self.
But one of them. Perhaps.
There are no guarantees even in the dark.

St. John of the Cross was a mystic, though he was never in Sedona.
He too had nice things to say about the night even if it was dark:

Oh, night that guided me,
Oh, night more lovely than the dawn,
Oh, night that joined Beloved with lover,
Lover transformed in the Beloved!

These Dark Nights of the Soul, Emily's closings, our empty bottles:
They keep getting connected to loving, leaving, being, transforming.
Emily told us, the death of the soul (a huge, hopeless to conceive closing)
    is all we know of heaven.
For her, too, the night could be good for the soul.

But Emily also says it is all we need of hell.
We NEED hell.
That is a BOLD idea.
We need hell to have heaven.
Hell is when the soul dies.
Hell is a time not a place.
If you cannot bear to lose something, it is hell to lose it.
Heaven to have it.

If you can bear to lose it, it is neither heaven to have nor hell to lose.

Heaven burns brightest when hell is on the horizon.
Once again Emily drives me to William.
To Sonnet 73 where death is "the glowing of such fire":

> In me thou see'st the glowing of such fire,
> That on the ashes of his youth doth lie,
> As the death-bed, whereon it must expire,
> Consum'd with that which it was nourish'd by.
> This thou perceiv'st, which makes thy love more strong,
> To love that well, which thou must leave ere long

Our soul dies when what we cherish leaves, parts, dies.
Such huge, hopeless to conceive events are the ultimate trackers of the
     human soul.
So is dreading them, often in the dark of night, a mini-death.
Our bottle is empty then.
All the milk is gone.
But we just might find more milk.
Though in the dark night we don't think so.
There is hope until the fire is out.

What if we stay empty?
What if we can find nothing more to cherish?
In my old days, when I was young, there was one and only one sin that
     could not be forgiven.
It was called the sin against the Holy Ghost (later known as the
     Holy Spirit).
It was suicide, the absence of hope.

But it always seemed to me, even back then, that the worst sin was denying
     others,
Or not supplying others,

Hope;
Which is to say,
Making it hard or impossible for them to find things to cherish.

Our soul is the part of us that can die more than once.
It is the part of us that can come back to life.
Like vampires recovering from their wounds in the dark.
It is, as Emily says, our immortality.

The soul is not chemical, because it is not inside us.
It is a bond between us and something else, something cherished.
What is cherished on the other end of the bond is not in us.
When the bond breaks—or is about to break—we see what we cherish
    in its clearest brightest light.
That's what William said.
And we die. Our life closes.
That's what Emily said.
Then, perhaps, it opens again.

It seems to me that the soul IS a fit academic topic.
How can we cherish the world and others before it is too late?
How can we give all people hope when they have died for a time?
How can we fill their bottles again with milk?
And won't that fill ours, too?

Fire at Night

Joe was a very old man in an old world.
He was fat and had thick glasses.
He wore all black.
And taught algebra.

He could barely see.
When I wrote my exam in pencil,
He couldn't see it.
"Mr. Gee, you give me nothing, I give you nothing," he wrote alongside
    my 'F'.

He liked to sit at his old wooden desk,
And make the students chant my name as fast as they could.
"Jim Gee!", "Jim Gee!", "Jim Gee!", they chanted while he pounded out
    each beat on the desk with his chalk bottle.
He liked that my name was short and you could say it fast.

We did algebra problems at the board.
He told us we must draw x's one way and not the other.
I made my x wrong, the way the Nuns had told us to in grade school.
He said, "Mr. Gee, that's not how we makes x's here".

I did it again and he covered me in chalk head to toe,

Pounding me slowly with a large dusty chalk eraser.
I have never made x's any way since save his.
That's mainly what I learned in Algebra class.

Larry was another very old man in the same old world.
He was tall but stooped and crippled, standing with the aid of two canes.
He wore all black.
And lectured from behind a wooden podium atop a stage.

We were afraid of him.
It was rumored that there was a blood stain next to the desk in his room.
I saw it once when I was called to see him, at least I think I did.
They said he had hit a wayward student with one of his canes.

In class, we sat in old wooden desks with chairs attached.
One day my friend Paul whispered to another student.
Larry dropped his canes and leapt from the stage,
Picked up the desk, with Paul in it, and carried it out the door,
And threw it into the courtyard below, Paul and all.

Of course we were all shocked.
I was shaking because I had thought Larry was coming for me.
None of us ever talked in class again.
And we believed all the more devoutly in the blood stain on the floor.

John was yet another very old man in that old world.
He was tall and absent minded.
He wore all black.
He taught two different classes
And carried a book with the names of his students in it everywhere.

He started each class by calling attendance from his book.
As he called each name, the designated student said "Yes".

But John usually called the names from the other class.
We each said yes anyway and John went happily on.

One day John was on a roll, oblivious we were there.
He was talking about a story in the Bible.
He said, "If you squeeze an orange, what do you get?"
"Orange juice".

Then he said, "If you squeeze a human being, what do you get?"
He stopped, said nothing more, and went on to something else.
Human being juice?
I didn't know then, but I do know now, what he meant.

Bucky was a very old man too in that old world.
He was very frail.
He wore all black.
He called on each of us in turn to translate Greek out loud.

I honestly believed Bucky had known Plato.
He was that old.
He sat silently after we each recited our Greek.
And just wrote a grade we never saw in an old book.

I was no good at Greek.
So to pass the exams I just memorized the English.
And tried to line it up with whatever Greek showed up on the test.
It was easier than actually learning Greek.

On one exam, Bucky gave me an 'A'.
He even wrote "Good job, Mr. Gee".
But, then, he wrote, "It is odd that there is one more paragraph of English
    than there is of Greek".
I had gone too far, missing where the Greek had actually ended.

A bonfire raged in the dark cloister.
Hormones raged as well in young male bodies around the fire.
Teens dressed all in black.
Very young men in a very old world.
It was Easter Eve late at night.
A vigil waiting for the Resurrection.
We went to Midnight Mass.
And then drank hot chocolate together in the old large drafty refractory.

That world is long dead.
And it will have no resurrection.
It died when the fire went out.
An old man myself now, in the Dark Night I seek kindling I cannot find.

Enough

Sadly, when you are old, enough is never enough.
Enough is less than you want.
More than you need.
But maybe enough is never enough even for the young.

An old folk tale has guest after guest come in.
Each asks if there is enough.
The gracious hostess always says, "There's just enough".
Enough never becomes less than enough.

Even for the wild young, enough runs out quickly.
For the old it runs out quicker still.
For the hostess enough is always just enough.
For me just enough is just too little.

If I have more than enough will others have too little?
Can some have more without others having less?
I get that less is more and moral,
If not everyone gets enough.

But not with wine.
Or food.
Or sex.

Or beauty.

Surely there is enough for all: Wine is not oil, we can grow grapes.
Food is not a gem, we can grow grain.
Sex only requires someone else and God knows there are plenty of them.
And beauty seems limitless.

But what of love?
Is there a shortage of that?
Can we grow love?
Is there enough--even more than enough--for every one?

Are we searching for love,
Searching even to love ourselves,
When enough is not enough?
Or is that a trite truth?

Is the truth in wine deeper?
That love is so rare,
We drink to wait and hope.
Until, if ever, enough is enough.

Book Two

Dad

Dad

They look at me askance.
I would have thought it was "a skance".
But that is why they look at me so.

I rarely heard fancy words at home.
Once I heard "pluralism" at the dinner table though.
Because my father read Hans Kung.

I only heard big words from theology books.
That's all my father ever read.
He taught himself to read Teilhard de Chardin autodidactically

My father told me he was thrown out of school in the third grade.
For climbing a flag pole in Mississippi.
He left home at thirteen and got through the Great Depression working
    at hotels in Kansas City.

He joined the 82nd Airborne, parachuting into World War II.
Broke his collar bone on the drop into Normandy and fought on.
Only late in life, near death, would he finally talk about the horror
    of the war.

Overseas he met an English girl from Derby.
After the War he took her to a cabin in the wilds of the Uvas.
Wolves howled and she demanded to move to the city.

Before the War he had started a taxi company in San Jose.
He returned to take it back from thugs.
Battling them with machine guns in the yard.

He was the first in town to hire African-Americans,
And he refused service ever again to anyone who wouldn't ride with them.
One day an African driver (not an African-American) who had not been
    driving long drove his cab into a plate glass window.

The store called to complain about the driver and the broken window.
They never got a cab again.
Dad had principles without nuances.

He wanted to choose a religion.
Pamphlets over-filled a drawer at home.
Like many uneducated people, he believed reading was a doorway to
truth.

A Jesuit named Father Ring passed by the cab company each morning
    on his way to Church.
Each day Dad doffed his hat and said, "Good day, Father".
Father Ring converted him to Catholicism and made his War Bride
    a bride again.

Dad petitioned Rome to annul a former marriage that had ended
    in divorce,
So he could marry Mom for "real" in the Catholic Church.
My identical twin brother and I, little boys dressed all in white, walked
    down the aisle throwing petals on the ground.

He developed a deep fondness for the Little St. Teresa and the Big one too.
Old as he was, he was an altar boy early each morning at Mass where the
    Carmelite nuns chanted, hidden behind a wall.
They could not venture out and spoke to visitors only from behind
    a wooden turnstile.

When my brother and I made our First Communion, we saw the nuns
    sitting in a bare room with cold iron bars.
They removed their veils so we could see their faces.
This was something they could do only for innocents making their
    First Communion.

I remember them still.
Frozen in time and place even then.
Old and young, virgins and innocents, they laughed and looked happy
    and well.

Dad thought we had looked on the faces of angels.
He would never see any of these women, women who he served for
    a lifetime,
Until he was on his death bed and they came to wish him well on his
    way to see the face of God.

When Dad died, Mom still went to the Carmelite Monastery for Mass.
One day in the courtyard she went off to watch a squirrel play in a tree.
Surprised I ran up to her and she gasped at the attention I had brought
    on her from others.

My mother hated public attention.
She could not stand to stand out.
When her life was drawing to a close, people stared at her in public while
    she fought the ill effects of an aneurism.

Like my mother, I have always hated people looking at me.
But when I ventured out,
They looked at me askance.

One day, Dad decided we would all go to Spain to trace the history of
    the Carmelites.
And a very long history it was.
Some said it started even before Christ, in the Holy Land on Mt. Carmel.

We visited my elderly grandmother in England first.
And my mother's many brothers and sisters.
I had never seen my English Grandmother; in fact she is the only
    Grandparent I ever saw.

My brother and I showed up in cowboy hats and boots, sporting toy rifles.
We guarded the front door of the old red brick house.
And watched horse drawn carts deliver bottles of milk.

Grandma's house had no refrigerator and no heat save from the
    kitchen stove.
She walked to town several miles each morning to buy the food for
    the day.
A small gray lady ambling with her bags to town, she lived a long
    long time.

Dad wanted to surprise Grandma with her first spaghetti dinner.
He went all over Derby looking for what turned out to be in England
    rare ingredients.
Grandma said it looked like worms and wouldn't eat it.

For reasons I do not know, my Anglican relatives ate fish on Friday just
    like us Catholics.
They did not know why either.

And denied there was any Irish in their line despite suspicions about
their name.

At night the house was frigid.
After a late supper of fish and chips wrapped in old newspaper, we ran
upstairs as fast as we could from the warm kitchen through the icy
house to bed.
God be praised, Grandma had placed a hot-water bottle under the stone
cold bed clothes.

Derby was a village then.
Old red brick houses and horse-drawn carts on cobbled roads.
Grandma had an outhouse and no indoor plumbing.

When Mom was nearing death, sick of the modern world, she longed to
return home to Derby.
To the Derby which she dreamed was there still.
We did not have the heart to tell her it was gone, transformed into an
industrial slum.

Though Dad had fought the Fascists in the War, we went to the Fascist
Franco's Spain.
Franco was a Catholic who heard Mass each day.
For Dad, that meant he had a good soul.

The desk clerks at the hotel offered to pay my brother and me to talk to
them in English.
They had learned British English and wanted to talk fast like us Americans.
Dad made us go down each night and talk for free.
The young bellhops knew no English and we knew no Spanish.
But they took us out each day to play with paper planes and such.
Language was no barrier for play.

We were surprised to see policemen stop all the cars and pedestrians to
    let us pass alone.
They asked us if they could take our picture in the middle of the road.
Finally, my Dad asked "Why?"

"We know who you are", the policeman said.
My father said, "Who am I then?"
"You're Eisenhower".

The paper had said Eisenhower was visiting Spain.
Dad looked like Ike.
To this day there are pictures still on Spanish mantles of Eisenhower and
    his two fat twins.

As we walked the streets of Spain, Dad found the passing priests uncivil.
Each time he doffed his hat and said with a smile "Good day,
    Father", they just walked by.
Not like the priests back home, not like dear old Father Ring.

One day, Dad had had it.
When an old priest walked silently by, Dad called out to him "What's
    this?" "Why so rude? Why just walk by?"
The old priest stopped and said, "Who are you?" meaning "Who in
    the Hell are you?

Dad said "I am Ernie Gee from San Jose California".
The old priest just stopped and thought.
Then he said, "Do you know a Jesuit by the name of Harold Ring?"

The old priest and Father Ring had attended the same seminary together
    long ago in Rome.
They were old friends who had not seen each other ever since.
Dad said Father Ring had converted him.

The old priest and my father became fast friends.
They toured Spain together looking at churches and buying old statues.
The old priest sent a Christmas card each year thereafter.

Dad was searching for the true Carmelites.
The ones who went way back to the Saints Teresa and beyond.
But at convent after convent he heard tales of theological fine points.

Petty differences.
"Well, really, Mr. Gee we are not quite like that other house".
It had been a forked and twisted path from old Mt. Carmel.

This was Old Europe and the Church after all.
For thousands of years Carmelites, both monks and nuns, had championed
    their own devotions.
Though they all reported to the Father General in Rome, there were
    nonetheless old and subtle differences.

Finally, Dad had had it (again).
Footsore and weary, he sought refuge in the sacristy of an old church.
Sitting on a bench he complained to us about "these Carmelites" in not
    so decent terms.

A monk came in tired too,
Unnoticed, he sat behind us.
Eventually he tapped my father on the shoulder.

He said, "I see you are unhappy with the Carmelites".
"Who are you?" meaning "Who are you, for heaven's sake?"
"I am Ernie Gee from San Jose, California".

The monk said, "I am the Father General of the Carmelites,
I am here from Rome on a visit to Spain".

They became fast friends and he sent a Christmas card each year thereafter.

We came home with lots and lots of slides.
My father, camera round his neck and family in tow, was what they then
    called "an Ugly American".
Pushing across Old Europe with naïve faith and unabashed forwardness.

Little did we know how truly ugly Americans would later get,
When they were not fresh off the beaches of Normandy,
But policing the world in the name of "American Exceptionalism".

Dad did not live all that long, he died at 52.
His people were Dust Bowl wanderers and they all died young.
An altar boy to the end, a series of heart attacks eventually felled him.

The Father General of the Carmelites in Rome cabled the nuns in
    California.
Make a habit and bury him as a Carmelite he said.
My brother and I, then in a monastery world ourselves, were allowed to
    attend his funeral where he lay in an open casket, in a monk's habit,
    gone to join the long line of Carmelites where he belonged.

Finally, I ventured out, out to the modern world.
They looked at me askance.
And have ever since.

I would have thought it was "a skance".
But that is why they look at me so.
I never heard fancy words at home.

Except that word "pluralism" which impressed me then even though
    I was quite young.
I lived in a closed world then and this magic word seemed to say there

were plural worlds in one society.
E pluribus unum, out of many, one, many devotions beyond my own.

I have lived a long time in that pluralistic society.
Its elites seem to live in as closed worlds as I once did.
They look at me askance.
Like my mother, I want to go home, but I know it's gone.
I can still hear, but barely, the chanting of the nuns,
And see my father kneeling at the altar of their song.

Sin

I was seven years old, the age of reason.
The age when for the very first time sin becomes possible.
Even necessary.

When I made my First Confession, I had to find a sin.
To prove I had the capacity to reason.
Or rather the common human capacity to have reason overridden
    by desire.

It's hard to sin when you're seven, at least back then when children were
    still children.
I hadn't done anything bad.
Not because I didn't want to, but because my father wouldn't let me.

No matter: For Catholics, wanting to do bad things was already a
    bad thing.
Wanting to do bad got you credit for doing it.
So I confessed to wanting to talk back.

I wonder now why thinking bad things gets you credit for being bad.
But thinking good things doesn't get you credit for being good.
To get credit for being good, you actually have to do good things.

For teens, having impure thoughts was a common sin.
It was hard to tell the priest the number though.
There were too many and they were difficult to individuate.

There were venial and mortal sins.
Venial sins got you time in Purgatory.
Mortal sins got you an eternity in Hell.

Sex outside marriage was a mortal sin.
So was murder.
Letting kids starve all over Africa wasn't.
It might seem that confession should have worked the other way round.
People should have told the priest what good things they had
     actually done.
"Father, I have not done any good at all, I have nothing to confess".

A focus on sin leaves too many people locked in thought and not deeds.
It leads to spending too much time removing sin from one's soul.
And not enough time removing harm and evil from the world.

Being good comes to mean avoiding sin and temptation.
Don't do this and don't do that.
But, would not God think well of a head full of dirty thoughts and a life
     full of good deeds?

Some Christians attack abortion clinics and that's a deed.
Yet they want to cut social services and champion the death penalty.
They do good things for embryos, not for real people.

There is a paradox about good deeds: They can only make things
     better, not perfect.
Evil flourishes in perfection.
Too often many die so that all can live.

Of course there are good Christians, Christ was one.
He told us not to cling to riches or status.
And To DO what he DID.

Christ made the final exam open book.
He gave out the questions well before he demanded the answers.
For some reason he left abortion off the test.

Come, you blessed of My Father,
Inherit the kingdom prepared for you
From the foundation of the world;

For I was hungry and you gave me food,
I was thirsty and you gave Me drink,
I was a stranger and you took Me in,

I was naked and you clothed Me,
I was sick and you visited Me,
I was in prison and you came to Me.

Assuredly, I say to you,
Inasmuch as you did it to one of the least of these My Brethren,
You did it to Me.

So there are only six questions on the exam.
The exam you get at the End of Time.
Hungry thirsty strangers and naked sick prisoners, that's all there is.

As we debate abortion and Christ in politics,
As we claim the U.S. is a Christian country, but that helping the poor is
    Communism,
I wonder about "Christians" who fail a test that was released ahead of time.

I visited a girlfriend in prison once.

I have unclothed more people than I've clothed.

But unlike "Christians" I don't claim to have passed the final exam.

I don't worry anymore about whether I am a good Christian.

The exam questions have settled that.

Old now, though, I wonder whether what little good I thought I did was
any good at all.

There is another exam I fear.

At the moment of death, when there is no reason left to lie even to
yourself, you ask:

"What good did I DO?"

Lies

It' s a lie.
What?
I forget.
I can only vaguely recall.

So many lies my brain is numb.
I can see just a glimpse.
But of what?
There are too many lies to remember.

Big lies, medium lies, little lies.
A Goldilocks of lies.
Some are just right.
Lulled to sleep by lies.

People lie to win.
People lie to keep others happy.
People lie to survive.
People lie to help and to harm.

We bathe in lies.
The media lies.
The politicians lie.

We all lie.

Why?
Because we want power, sex, and money.
Because we want respect.
Because we want love.
Because we want to belong, not to be left alone.

Lies lubricate social life.
Lies negotiate the peace and start the wars.
Lies allow us to sleep at night.
In the morning, lies allow us to get up and go on.

We cannot stop lying and believing lies.
We are addicted to lies.
They keep the world at bay.
And lock us into the battered shelter of self-deception.

But what is there out there that frightens us so?
The indifferent universe.
And people in a zero sum game.
A game only one of us can win.
A cage fight to the end.

People claim to like us, to be our friend, even to love us.
But they just need warmth against the cold.
And we need a companion by the fire.
When the fire goes out we are alone again.

We seek.
We weep.
We wish.
We fail.

In desperation we come to the communal fire.
To whoop with the tribe.
To pump ourselves up for violence.
Against the others who otherwise we would love.

We are frail beasts.
Evolved from creatures that ate or got eaten.
We awoke with consciousness one day and pain became suffering.
Then we all desperately sought a lie that would make everything all right.

Big Experience: Presidential Election, November 6, 2012

I have written a lot about experience.
We used to think that the mind was made of rules and calculations.
But it is made first and foremost of patterns found in lived experience.
We use these patterns as bets and guides for future decisions and actions.

The old scout sits in the stands.
"I've done this for 30 years".
"I know 'em when I see 'em".
"That guy's a keeper".

Now a quant runs some numbers.
Numbers originally dreamed up by amateur baseball fanatics.
The numbers say he's not a keeper.
And he's not.

Alan Greenspan says "I've been doing this for 40 years".
"I've run this economy for a long time".
"I know my markets".
"I know business and business is the business of America".

The global economy tanked in 2008, thanks to Al and US.
Alan said "I never saw it coming".
In fact, he had advised people to trade in their fixed mortgages for
    balloon payments.
He had said the price of houses would never fall.

Alan went to Congress after the collapse.
"Nothing in my 40 years of economics told me this would happen".
"I believed that free markets always give rise to the best outcomes".
"I believed CEOs would never purposely harm the companies they run".

But Alan! There were no free markets.
You deregulated them.
Frost said you cannot play tennis without a net.
Alan, you removed the referees and were surprised the thugs cheated.

But Alan! The CEO's companies were "companies" no more.
You thought a company made something that made profit.
But now companies are just holds for quick bets on their stock price.
Bet now and get out quick before customers find out no one cares what
    the company makes.

The quant guys with their Big Data ran the numbers.
Alan, they knew it was a House of Cards and it was all going to fall.
The smart guys on the Street took the short bets and got vastly richer yet.
The "little" guys saw their houses, families, and lives blow away.

Karl Rove fell apart on Fox News when Ohio was called for Obama.
"It can't be so", he said.
"I've done this for many many years".
"I was Bush's Brain".
"I know there are Red Votes still out there. I just know it".

But Karl missed the Puerto Ricans moving into the Red county in Florida.
He missed demographic changes that had been predicted and in motion
　　since the 1970's.
He missed facts of human nature:
Trying to stop people from doing something (voting) makes them want
　　to do it more.
Insulting people doesn't make them want to vote for you.
You can't buy votes unless you buy the voters.
Money to ad companies and television channels won't cut it.
And you don't buy the voters by knocking down their wages.

The quant guys ran their algorithms and massaged their data seven ways
　　to Sunday.
They said here is how the election will go.
And that is just how it went.
And the people on Fox looked like someone had killed their dog.
Nate Silver called the election.
He had started as an amateur baseball stats guy.

Numbers are dangerous, of course.
Algorithms on computers now buy and sell stocks on the fly at warp speed.
There is the danger they will all get in synch and sink the market.
Getting in synch is what complex systems often do, like fireflies.

But numbers are benignly indifferent, too.
They don't care that the catcher is bald.
They don't care that Puerto Ricans moved in.
They don't care that the Alan and Karl are powerful, elite, old, and sad.
Numbers are humane or, at least, tolerant.

The problem is that experience isn't what it used to be.
Experts are people with credentials who have had lots of experience.
But even a vast amount of experience is a small sample in the face of
　　Big Data.
And credentials are for being good at one narrow thing.

Yet the important stuff today is all about many complex interactions.
Today, the expert's one thing is soon gone or vastly changed anyway.
Furthermore, amateurs on the Web can now beat experts at their own
   game.

But, alas, experience is the foundation of human learning and intelligence.
We build our knowledge on the basis of patterns we have found in our
   experience.
We make our choices on the basis of patterns we have found in our
   experience.
No experience, no knowledge—we are left with only words floating free
   from the world.
But now that Big Data trumps experience, we can all look like someone
   killed our dog.

Big Data can level the proud and humble alike.
But numbers have their limits.
They can predict what will happen,
But they cannot say what should happen.

To trump Big Data—to tame it for the good—we need Big Experience.
Yours and mine alone will no longer do.
We need to pool our experiences.
To get diverse minds and souls in synch, like fireflies.
To make everyone count.
To seek out the mutant, the odd man out.
To find the datum Big Data will never find,
Because it is just the odd thing one person saw or felt,
A thing too small to see and too big to miss.

On the savannah, as we evolved, human experience was usually veridical
   because the world was small.
But today our world is big and out experiences of it is small and limited.
Our unaided minds—no matter how expert we are—are no good anymore.
Big Data will always show us the world does not fit our preconceptions.

But Big Data will face the same problem the Social Sciences have always
     faced.
Humans can make things true by willing and doing them.
They can change the Data.
Unlike an atom they pay attention to what is said about them.

The question is: What should we make?
We can make more than ever before with Fab Labs soon to be as prevalent
     as computers at home.
We can make change through networks and social media outside the
     strictures of institutions.
We will soon be able to make worlds as easily as we can now destroy them.
     But what will we make?
Will we save the planet only to make hell on earth, perhaps even by trying
     to make heaven on earth?
When you can make Karl Rove cry, what will you do next?

Collective Intelligence
Wisdom of the Crowd
Crowd Sourcing
Synchronized Minds
Shared Minds
Networked Intelligence
Distributed Intelligence
It's all Big Experience, the mental analogue of Big Data
Let's hope it is wiser than our savannah minds have been.

Choices

A fork in the path.
I turn left.
Now I will always be "the person who turned left when he could have
    turned right".

A fork in the path.
I am blown right by a strong wind.
Now I will always be "the person who was blown right when he might
    have chosen otherwise".

After a great many twists and turns,
I become "the person who turned or was blown right left left right right
    right left …. when it could or might have all been otherwise".
Our lives and ourselves turn into a circuitous route composed of when
    and where there was a chosen or a forced turn.

Sometimes we just let the wind choose,
And go wherever even a gentle wind bids us,
Three sheets to the wind even when we're not drunk.

We cannot always tell if we chose or were blown.
And surely we often cannot remember.
Does it matter in a game where you cannot turn back?

Long ago in a trailer in a forest I made a bad choice.
That choice forced another and another.
Now I regret the first choice but I am what I am now from all the others.

What if I could go back and make that choice again?
It would not be me that goes back to decide again.
I am the ill formed progeny of that choice, no longer the innocent I once
      was.

It would be that long-gone innocent making the new choice.
But that innocent would soon become something else altogether once
      the new choice was made.
That innocent self, even if wise enough to make a different choice, or
      let the wind choose, would now be a route I never took and utterly
      unrecognizable to me as me.

How would he judge me? How would I judge him?
What could the judgment of or by an alternative self really mean?
Is this what the Final Judgment at the Gates of Heaven is?

What are people who read self-discovery books seeking to discover?
They say they want to know who they are.
Better, I think, if you are young, to seek who you should be, though it
      won't be what you become.

When you are old, you no longer want to know who you are,
Or who you should be,
But what you have become and what you should think of it.

Is the proper emotion guilt?
Regret?
Loathing?
Or surprise?

Shrines

A thick forest of gloom.
A small shrine of stone.
A rotting log by a cold fire.
I sit alone on the log staring at the last shrine.

Shrines have propelled the human race.
Each group constructs a shrine for devotion to its chosen god,
Expecting favors in return.
But sooner or later the shrine always runs dry.

The favors cease.
The devotion wanes.
Skeptics arise.
Then someone notices that the shrine next door still seems to work.

Those foreigners next door,
Just far enough away not to have occasioned a war,
But just close enough to borrow and steal from now and then.
Appear to have the real thing.

Their shrine works.
Their gods really do listen and reward.
Our shrine is bogus.

So let's adopt theirs.

The new shrine works for a while.
Then it too runs dry.
We spy yet another and adopt it.
But that one too will soon run dry and we will seek another again.

Religions and myths have always borrowed and stolen.
They become mixed and mired in each other.
Some religions wrote books to stop it.
But even books as shrines run dry no matter what.

Does the god desert the shrine?
Or was he never there?
Do our devotions eventually fail to please him?
Or do our devotions merely fool us?

We humans need something to worship.
We need an insurance policy against chance and fate.
An insurance policy against a short life and a bad death.
But the company never pays.

Each of us, no matter how modern, erects shrine after shrine in our
    personal lives.
Shrines to forces that we hope can save us,
Shrines to money, fame, fortune, family, nations, and many other lesser
    gods.
But these shrines all run dry too.

All the altars where I have worshipped are barren now.
As all shrines do, they have run bone dry.
I wait patiently now for the last god to come through the forest of gloom
To sit beside me near the cold fire at my final shine.

Book Three

Love and Puds

Caring

I am a member of the "I Don't Give a Fuck Anymore Club",
A 12 step program for people who once cared.
Caring brought us stress, anxiety, anger, and disdain.
It destroyed us and those we cared about as well.

John cared about his job and was forced to train his own replacement.
Mary cared about her husband and got replaced by a young male.
Fred cared about the environment and now they frack in his backyard.
Sue cared about her cat who moved in next door.

Caring is toxic to the soul.
You suffer every hurt of someone else,
And every setback to a cause,
When you have your own private suffering to bear.

To care about an institution is the stupidest thing.
Institutions are designed to squander any opportunity for good.
They are full of people who claim to follow rules for the greater good,
But only as a ruse to suck the greater good dry for their own benefit.

Oh, yes, humans do follow one general rule,
"To thine own self be true".
But it means "Screw others if you need to,

And pretend to care if you must".

"The I Don't Give a Fuck Anymore Club" is for people who were foolish
    enough to care.
They thought the cause was all about the cause, but it never was.
They thought the institution was all about its vaunted goal, but it wasn't.
They thought others cared, but they really didn't.

The "I don't give a fuck anymore" state is liberating.
You can feel your arteries opening.
Your muscles relaxing.
And your heart closing.

You long to say, "No, I don't care,
You have mistaken me for someone else.
Here's a quarter, call someone who still cares.
I don't give a fuck, not even a flying fuck, whatever that is".

I could have been a great success had I cared less.
I could have lived longer.
I could have lived lighter.
I have aged beyond my years by adding worry about others to worries
    about myself.

Now I am facing an early grave.
Caring has caused my telomeres to fray.
The people, the causes, and the Institutions I cared about have moved on.
My care meant little and accomplished even less.

Now don't mistake me and think I care what you think,
Or that I claim any merit by having been addicted to care.
Caring is the rare disease that has no Internet support group.
It's a disease everyone wants to claim, but no one wants to have.

We in the "I Don't Give a Fuck Anymore Club" don't have sponsors.
To sponsor someone else would require caring.
We go it on our own.
There's no one to call if we lapse back and give a damn.

I often wonder who started our group,
Since that would have required caring about us all.
All that is known is that the founder passed on worn down by care,
A failure in the eyes of the club who can't remember his name.

We care addicts were raised by parents who bought the scam that
    people care,
When what they really care about is only themselves and their kin.
We all wonder now how our parents ever got old enough to mate,
When evolution should have taken care of them long before.

A meeting of the club is a cold affair.
There's no hugging and no support.
We take our turns admitting errors.
But no one cares.

De Rerum Natura

A Western Grebe bobs gently on the sea
Then darts below
And breaks the surface with a small silver fish
Swallowed in a flash.

Casual death
Every moment of every day of every year
For billions of years
De Rerum Natura.

A cat pounces on a bird
That flutters and dies
As the cat enters the magic circle
Of play.

The torturer water boards his foe
Who gasps and gasps for air
Inside the magic circle
Of pain.

An institutionalized child screams
While "an alternative asset management firm" fires caretakers
To raise stock prices
And make rich people richer.

A girl has acid thrown in her face
Because quite reasonably
She doesn't want to marry a man
Who would throw acid in her face.

A toddler slips and falls
Through space
In the flash of a parent's eye
And is murdered by gravity.

Good and bad people alike cry out for reasons
From an all-powerful all-knowing all-good God
Who, they say, tells them it's all for good
And meant to be.

I don't buy it
Because I don't want to worship a God
Who would let acid destroy a young girl's face.
Even if he had a good reason.

"Beware of false prophets
Who come to you in sheep's clothing
But inwardly are ravenous wolves.
By their fruits you will know them".

Lies of Hope

We beg for the mercy of lies
So we don't have to face the mercilessness of truth.
But one day we wake up and swear to tell the truth,
And then have no idea what it is.

There are hand-caught-in-the-cookie-jar lies
Which never work.
And there are cowardly lies,
Sins we inevitably pay for long before we get to the Pearly Gates.

There are lies of arrogance.
When we assume we know the truth and hide it.
Indeed we thought that's what it meant to lie.
But in reality we had no idea what the truth was and only kidded ourselves
    we did.

There are also lies of hope.
Where we aren't so much lying
As improvising,
Trying to hit a moving target we cannot always see.

At their best our lies are hopes,
Try outs

For an improvisational play
We cannot script.

I regret the lies I told.
But often I knew no truths any better.
Some of the lies I told came true and made the world better.
And some were just lies that made the world all the worse.

Now I face the Final Judgment.
The choir of angels tells me there were truths I should have known.
And I would dearly love to have known what they were.
So I improvise and tell the angels my best lies were guesses in the dark,
Mapping the maze bump by bump.

As for my worst lies,
I throw myself on the mercy of the court
And hope they lie to me
And tell me it's all all right.

Tower in Ruins

Why is the tower in ruins?
Deep down in its darkest dungeon
We kept a secret that would not stand the light.

We were in the tower to worship knowledge, not God or gods.
But we were priests nonetheless
And made sacrifices at our altar.

Our sacred duty was to expose false gods,
To face facts rather than to create myths,
To root out superstitions.

To do so we withdrew into our monastery
And made pronouncements ex cathedra
To a world that rarely cared.

When we brought them new cures
Or new tech toys and other magical tools,
They cared for the things but not the theories.

Our words were stale.
They inspired neither hope nor fear,
But only boredom.

We unlocked the secrets of the universe
And made impossible bombs that actually went off.
But late at night some people wanted to know what it meant to be here.

Science sometimes made life better.
And sometimes it made it worse.
But science didn't give life meaning or worth.

The peons in the tower were the ones who were supposed to work on that.
They were to meditate on the meaning of it all
With paint brushes, stories, poems, and philosophical tracts.

But they sought tenure and merit increases more fiercely
Than they sought the meaning of things.
When the tower became a business they had nothing to sell.

The peons announced the death of meaning and stories and "theory".
They told the laity they were all dupes,
Not even modern enough to be postmodern.

We all, scientists or not, published not to perish
Good work was lost in a sea of trash
The vast majority of it never cited.

We were all too busy going to conferences
And writing things no one read
To remove the trash or teach the acolytes.

The tower became a business.
We sold what we had claimed was beyond price
And discovered it wasn't worth all that much on the open market.

Competitors came from all sides.
E-learning spread our kitschy knick-knacks everywhere
And amateurs learned without us how to make live viruses in
    their kitchens.

We made our tower a job training center,
And told the rubes they'd all get good jobs,
As wages, income, equality, and dignity plummeted.

But what in the hell did we know about jobs?
Our tower was meant, we had said, to enable vocations,
To be about a calling, not a job.

We all bemoaned the day our tower became a business center,
Just another type of insurance scam.
But we had been selling status all along.

We weren't making people better.
We were making better off people better off.
And warehousing the less well off in the less well off towers.

We claimed audaciously that books had power,
But in reality we offered credentials and other trinkets,
That were no better than indulgences or superstitions.

We eventually found it was cheaper just to sell them
Rather than make anyone work to earn them,
Since they didn't mean anything anyway.

Now we have courses with 50,000 students
Earning certificates that are special
Only because they're not really as real as the other unreal ones we give.

We have "for profit" diploma mills,
No better than check cashing stores in rundown neighborhoods,
Offering students debt, lies, and bad degrees.

Catholic priests abused children sexually
And earned scorn.
We abuse them intellectually and earn money.

What was the secret in the dark dungeon deep?
What was there that turned to ashes in the light?
That we were meant to be priests of meaning, not just knowledge.

Meaning is hard and not for sale.
We can only baptize you when you begin the search
And bury you when you're dead.

Not all needed or wanted the search,
Many are happy just as they are,
The tower was for those willing to sacrifice happiness for meaning.

The secret that died in the dungeon
Was that we had abandoned our birthright there.
The light showed us for what we had become.

We sacrificed our birthright on the altar in the dungeon downstairs.
Not ourselves.
Now we have paid the final price.

We are hirelings at a faux wood desk,
Writing bad checks on a drawn account,
With a quota to make.

Love and Puds

I am sorry I don't fit your conception
Of who I am
Or who I should be
Or who I could be.

I am sorry I offend you,
Because I am different people at different times,
A cheap schizophrenic,
Fueled by sadness, anger, mistaken friendship, hope, despair, and alcohol.

I am always impressed by how "academic liberals"
Who champion "diversity"
Have no tolerance for people like me
When we are not what they want us to be.

They disdain people for whom socializing is an Olympic event
A struggle just to finish.
They like people who are "diverse" in just the right way,
A way that makes the "liberals" feel good about themselves.

My love tells me:
"That's the good thing about puds,
They don't care".

That's why we have nine.

In a recent interview I was asked "Are you ever alone?"
I said "Never", never anymore.
I am always with my love and my puds.
We're all curled up on a big bed.

The judgers and the judgments fade away.
And I finish the race in my own way.
Not necessarily in a good way and surely not in a better way than anyone
    else's.
But in the way that was open to me.

Leading

I was never a leader.
A coward, I always sought to flee.
Retreats were never merely tactical for me.
But alas I have a terrible sense of direction.

Fleeing rapidly out the back,
I got lost and ended up at the front.
Brave men were fighting there against all odds,
Until they saw me running toward the foe.

They were cheered by my courage
And rushed into the breach,
Glad to follow a real leader
Whose terrified scream sounded like a battle cry.

When I saw the hostile troops,
I turned at once
To seek a quick escape
In what perhaps looked to be a feint to fool the foe.

I got spun around anew.
Running in the direction of what I thought was home,
I came upon the enemy's reinforcements rushing in.

Half my cadre followed me and easily won the day.

I ran off as fast I could, but was soon adrift again.
At last I heard shouts of victory and joy,
And was hailed a returning hero as I magically appeared,
Lost and back where I had started from.

There the troops were regimented
To salute a leader bold and brave,
To give me a medal for finding the way
As I asked for directions from the fray.

Nature

Humans are intention seekers.
We see intention everywhere.
In light and shadow and shade.
In mountains, sky, and sea.

We cannot accept that the Red Rocks of Sedona
Or the red deserts of Australia
Were carved by old seas and erosion,
And not by the art of a godly sculptor.

We go further and feel it's all alive.
We stand in mountain vortexes swirling with special powers.
We hear breezes as messages
And sense the presence of ancients who painted symbols on the rocks.

I have walked through the Australian red deserts.
The landscape quivers with animateness,
The stones and dunes seem ever so slightly to move
As the rock kangaroos sit quietly on their mothers of stone.

We humans need to see the meanings of things
And hear the messages they send.
We cannot settle for the thingness of things

Including animate things like ourselves.

Do we redeem nature by giving it meaning
And deciphering its intentions?
What if javelinas and rock kangaroos have nothing to say,
Except that they are alive on their own terms?

We humans are trapped in the spider webs of meaning.
We can never be alive on our own terms.
We have to mean something everywhere and always
And our intentions have to be scrutinized constantly.

We cannot just be a thing full of thingness.
We have to have a soul
And maintain human progress
While we devastate the earth on our way to heaven.

I often fantasize sitting still in the Red Mountains,
Honoring nature as my goddess--
Then the mountain lion pounces

Music from Trash

Each silence fragments the soul.
Piece by piece it falls apart.

Now that I am old, my soul is melting away altogether,
Like a glacier calving in the Age of Global Warming.
Too little is left to hold out any longer against the toxins in the institutional
     air I breath.

I once thought old people grew old souls.
Now I know souls grow hard, freeze, and then finally melt away,
Hived off block by block by compromises we should not have made.

Soulless, I am left adrift in the detritus of my past,
Swimming in the backwash of the wreckage of my soul,
A backwash filled with the havoc my sins have wreaked.

What happens when the soul is gone?
What happens when it's all a sea filled with wreckage and debris?
What happens when we feel too old and hurt to swim to shore?

Souls ice over so we can get on by going along.
So we can bear the pain of stupidity.

Not stupid people, no not at all,
But forms of life that make us all unwise.

But perhaps from the litter in our soulless sea we can fabricate a new soul.
We can make from the garbage a new more fragile but angry soul.
Fragile because we always knew the kids who played symphonies with
    instruments made from trash were more worthy than the rich kids
    who padded their applications to Harvard with expensive instruments
    played with no passion.
But we kept silent.
Angry because we sacrificed our first soul on an altar to false gods.

Then perhaps we learn to swim through the mistakes of our past,
Ungainly,
Slowly,
Because we are "differently abled" now.

Redistribution: A Primer on 21st Century Economic Theory

A teacher wants to get across to her students the evils of redistribution.
She believes redistribution is a socialist, communist, liberal plot to
    undermine America.
It is a doctrine of moochers and takers not makers and shakers.
It makes people dependent and fails to "incentivize" them for success.

Redistribution is an out and out evil.
Unfair, unjust, immoral, and unconstitutional.
It undermines the very foundations of society.
It kills the desire to work hard for low wages.

"How fair would a grading system be that made the A's give points to the
    B's and C's and D's,
And, God forbid, even to the F's!", she says.
"That's how redistribution works.
The people who earned it have to give to those who didn't."

Of course, students in a course and people in America do not all start at
    the same starting line.
Some, with privileged backgrounds, start already many yards ahead.
Others start way behind the line.
The teacher calls it a fair race nonetheless.

Some earned their A through hard work,
But others earned their A by starting well ahead.
Some earned a C because they started way behind
And made more progress than any of the A's.

The teacher is right but in the wrong direction.
For the last many decades wealth in America has been redistributed up
    not down.
The rich have taken from the middle class and the poor,
And in the act have surpassed the Age of the Robber Barons.

The rich raided everyday people's bank accounts once Glass-Steagall
    was repealed.
They created a lucrative poverty industry out of payday loans, check
    cashing, and usurious credit cards.
They harvested companies by laying off workers, lowering wages, and
    raiding pension funds.
They made derivatives out of liar loans and foreclosed on homes.

They bought politicians, got subsidies, cut health care, and left the rest
    of us with the bill.
They claimed they had "earned it" when they had inherited wealth or
    had famous parents.
They demanded meritocracy for others but no inheritance tax for their
    kids so they would not have to compete.
They colluded to rig Libor rates and raise CEO pay, but decried unions.

They had the Supreme Court pass Citizens United so the corporations
    and the rich could steal elections.
They sought to restrict voting, just in case their money wouldn't turn
    the trick.
Then they claimed the election was stolen when they lost,
Because it was their God-given right to win.

So the teacher was confused about who the moochers were.
If redistribution is a Commie plot, then our rich are Commies through
    and through.
Though I suspect the teacher is happy with the rich taking from the rest
    of us,
After all, they're rich, so they MUST be smart, as any social
    Darwinist knows.

For our teacher, downward redistribution-- the sort Christ was for--
    is evil.
And upward redistribution is good, since when wealth trickles down
    to the poor the rich can take it again and "grow" the economy.
Our teacher probably calls herself a good Christian,
But she is in fact a devout Milton Friedmanian.

For the record, trickle down--supply side--economics is a fraud and
    economies grow by consumption.
Workers with no jobs or bad wages can't buy anything.
See, it had nothing really to do with morality but only with capitalism,
A system we should try.

In the 21st Century there is another case for downward redistribution
    beyond consumption.
It is a sort of Christian argument on steroids for helping those who have
    fallen behind.
Today our world is imperiled by complex systems and fierce conflicts.
The earth and the human species are challenged as never before.

You don't slay a dragon with an A.
It takes a team whose strength is no better than its weakest link.
Faced with the dragon's fire, you can bet that the best gives to the worst
    to get them up to speed,
Before the whole team is burnt to a crisp.

If you're a warrior fighting at the dragon's feet,
You don't ask whether the healer was once a slacker or deprived,
You damn well see to it he will be ready to save you when you are
    about to die,
And vice versa.

That's how to survive a major dungeon in the World of Warcraft.
And that's how the army takes a hill in a bloody battle in the desert, though
    in America rich kids don't go to war.
You redistribute your butt off until everyone is the best they can be.
The team becomes better, smarter, and sometimes braver than anyone in it

Then you don't just get a silly A, you gain victory.
The guild gives you the best drop.
And the army gives you a medal for saving not just yourself but all of us.
You earned it, but you couldn't have done it without the team.

The battle for the earth and for life on our planet,
For the survival of the human species,
Is already joined.
The dragon is at the gates.

Don't bring your A to the battle and brag about it,
Or your money and tell us how hard your parents worked to give it to you.
Bring the respect you won when you buffed your team mates so they
    could help you save the day.
When the dragon roars, you need people to watch your back, not admire
    your golden ass.

If you don't believe me, as I know you won't,
See what happens when you stand before the dragon alone and show
    him your A.
Tell him the others are not there because they didn't get an A.
As you perish, you might even scream, "It isn't fair, they weren't as good

as me".

Ah, but I hear you say, "I've got you now,
I will bring a team of only A's,
People all as good and smart as me.
People who toed the line and did what they were told".

Too bad you didn't know this particular dragon was impervious to a team
    of only standard skills.
What you really need now is that screwed up dwarf,
The one you earlier denied drops you really didn't need.
What he might have become is what you need now to save yourself.

"But, surely", you say, "Helping should be a matter of charity,
Not the government or the team telling me what to do".
You are right, you should not be forced on the team.
You can sit it out and hope those you wouldn't help will help you.

But perhaps I'm wrong,
And you'll be just fine,
Alone with your own kind.

A Christmas Poem

When they came for him in the garden,
He didn't stand his ground.
When Peter drew his sword and cut off the High Priest's slave's ear,
Christ healed the slave and ordered Peter to back down.

The rich would hate him as a guest at their fancy dinners.
He would invite prostitutes, tax collectors, lepers, and poor people in.
He would tell parables about how hard it is for the rich to get to heaven,
And how the first shall be last and the last shall be first.

If they bemoaned government, he would tell them to give unto Caesar
    what is Caesar's.
If they celebrated wealth, he would tell them to give all their wealth away.
If they decried the inheritance tax, he would tell them only the meek
    inherit the earth.
If they shouted "Don't Tread on Me", he would tell them to turn the
    other cheek.

They say America is a Christian nation.
They say Christ supports our wars,
They say we should see great wealth as a sign of grace.
I say these people might be wrong.

But today I won't stand my ground,
Merry Christmas.

About James Paul Gee

James Paul Gee was born in San Jose, California in 1948. He was raised a devote Catholic and attended a seminary for 5 years, starting at the age of 13. He received his PhD in linguistics in 1975 from Stanford University.

He has written and taught in a wide variety of areas, including syntactic theory, psycholinguistics, literary stylistics, sociolinguistics, discourse analysis, literacy studies, ASL linguistics, deaf education, learning theory, and digital media, with an emphasis on video games and learning. He has taught and been tenured at six different colleges and held three endowed chairs. He is currently the Mary Lou Fulton Presidential Professor at Arizona State University.

He loves nature and birding, and abhors the disrespect we humans have shown our world and each other. He writes poetry as the "spirit" moves him, not as an academic, but as an older human being who, like all old people, can see the face of death, the value of life, and the need to imagine and implement new and better worlds for all creatures, human and otherwise.

Books by James Paul Gee

Garn Press Books by James Paul Gee

Blowing Out the Candles: Book One – Souls (2013)

Blowing Out the Candles: Book Two – Dad (2013)

Blowing Out the Candles: Book Three - Love and Puds (2013)

Other Books by James Paul Gee

Social Linguistics and Literacies (1990)

The Social Mind (1992)

The New Work Order (1996), with Glynda Hull and Colin Lankshear

An Introduction to Discourse Analysis (1999)

What Video Games Have to Teach Us about Literacy and Learning (2003)

Situated Learning and Language (2004)

Why Video Games Are Good For Your Soul (2005)

Good Video Games and Good Learning (2007)

Women as Gamers (2010), with Elisabeth Hayes

How To Do Discourse Analysis (2010)

Language and Learning in the Digital Age (2011), With Elisabeth Hayes

The Anti-Education Era (2013)

www.ingramcontent.com/pod-product-compliance
Lightning Source LLC
Chambersburg PA
CBHW070316120726
47910CB00007B/2511

* 9 7 8 0 9 8 9 9 9 1 0 6 3 7 *